THE GREATEST WORLD
WE CAN MAKE IT TOGETHER

Written by
Janice Surlin

HOME SWEET HOME

Illustrated by
Madison Koslowski

I0196356

The Greatest World:
We Can Make It Together

For children and grown-ups and in-between too,
if you live on Earth this book's for you!

Text Copyright © 2020 by Janice Surlin
Illustrations copyright © 2020 by Madison Koslowski

All rights reserved. No part of this book may be reproduced or
transmitted in any form or by any means, electronic or mechanical,
including photocopying, recording, or by any information storage
and retrieval system, without permission from the publisher.

ISBN: 978-0-9981700-1-5

Published by Hummingbird Jewel Press
info@hummingbirdjewelpress.com

Dedicated To

Zachary, Allison, Brachi, Chava, Menachem,
who bring so much love and joy into *my* world,
and all children here, and yet to be,
who deserve to live in a kind, healthy world;
and
"grown-up" kids, Joshua, Jason, Jennifer,
for their enduring devotion, inspiration,
and graciously listening to my poems since childhood.
—J.S.

I would like to dedicate this book to my close friends and family,
and I especially wish to thank Grandma Bea for all of her
encouragement to keep working hard at what I love to do.
—M.K.

Author Acknowledgments

My profound admiration and special thanks to my gifted illustrator
for her amazing animal pictures and awesome cover.

My deep gratitude to Jennifer Galynsky for her beautiful book design and support.

And, to talented budding artists, Allison Galynsky and Brachi Lewis,
my great appreciation for illustrating the concluding poem verses and last page.

Preface

From the air we breathe
To the food we eat,
The Earth sustains life
In a system complete;
We humans and animals,
Plants, flowers and trees,
Depend on each other
From land, air, and seas—
The World is a Wonderful Home
For us all,
People and animals,
The big and the small!

The blue whale is the largest animal ever to have lived on Earth: the length of 3 school buses; heart the size of a small car; tongue weighing as much as an elephant.

Hummingbirds are tiny and the bee hummingbird is the smallest bird in the world: around 2 inches; able to fly 25 to 30 miles an hour.

Life is full of things to learn,
So much from "A" to "Z"—
Like fascinating animals
Rhymed alphabetically!

The animals you see in here
That fit this rhyming scheme,
Though rather large in number
To some of you may seem...
They really are a very few
Of all the animals who
Share with us our *Wonderful World*
And incredible *Web of Life* too!*

*Two animals in the poem do not fit this category:

Extinct dinosaurs: We are here thanks to the dinosaurs' disappearance. Unfortunate for them, but their extinction after dominating the Earth for over 150 million years paved the way for our existence.

Mythical white, horse-like unicorn: However, there once was a 3-1/2 ton "Siberian unicorn"—an Ice Age wooly rhinoceros-like animal with one huge horn. Believed to still have existed more recently than previously thought when 29,000-year-old fossils were discovered; humans who walked the Earth then really could have seen a unicorn!

Aardvarks

Alligators

Armadillos
so distinct

Bats, Baboons and Camels,
Ducks, and Dinosaurs extinct

Elephants and Foxes,
Tall Giraffes, great Gnus, of course

Hares
and
Hippopotami,

Whose name means "river horse"

Hummingbirds, such fun to watch,
They glitter as they fly,

Forward,   backward,   upside down

These tiny birds whiz by

Ibex, which are wild goats,
And Jaguars fast and sleek,
Kangaroos with pouches
From which little joeys peek

Lemmings, Lions, Llamas, Lynx and Leopards with black spots

Mockingbirds,
who copy sounds,
Minks, Newts
and Ocelots

Penguins, Peacocks, Pandas,
Porcupines with pointy quills

Porpoises and Quails,
Ringed Raccoons and Razorbills

Reindeer and Rhinoceri,
Skunks with uncommon scents

Toucans, Toads and Tortoises,
Known for their indolence*

*slowness

Tropical Umbrella Birds,
With forward curving crests

Unicorns, since mythical,
Make unobtrusive*guests

*unnoticeable

Vipers have their venom,
Voles resemble chubby mice

Walruses and Whippoorwills,
Whose songs are very nice

Whales are really mammals,
Weighing several tons at birth;
A baby blue grows up to be
The biggest animal on Earth

X-Ray fish are see-through,
Yorkshire terriers are cute,
Zebras look distinguished
In a black and white striped suit!

Yes, life is full of things to learn,
So much from A to Z,
But each of us must also learn
To live responsibly . . .

To treat each other kindly,
No matter where or who,
Will make the world a better place
For all of us, it's true!

Protecting our environment,
Respecting ALL creation,
Our World will be the Greatest Home
For every generation!

Whales and Hummingbirds

The next few pages are
especially intended for the
"grown-ups" and "in-betweens,"
mentioned on the cover, to enjoy
and share the facts they contain
with children in age appropriate
understanding.

Here you will see how the largest
and tiny animals affect the world,
each in their own way:

The blue (and other) whales,
playing a critical role in
producing Earth's life-sustaining
oxygen, and hummingbirds,
having a smaller but significant
role in the ecosystem. After all,
who can expect these tiny, dazzling,
incredible birds to save the world, or
would want to be without the wonder,
beauty, and joy they bring *to* the world!

It is a great testimony to the connectedness of life on earth that the fates of the largest and the tiniest life should be so closely dependent on each other.
—Steven Ben Johnson, Science Author

Whale Pods

What a group of whales is called—no connection to iPods.
A little humor about ENORMOUSLY important animals!

Not only is the blue whale the largest animal ever to have lived on Earth (and a most fascinating one to be sure), it is enormously important in helping the oceans produce, along with other whales, around 80% of the Earth's oxygen—earning them the title of *ecosystem engineers*. It definitely is not an overstatement that every person and animal is dependent on the oceans for every breath of air, and you soon will see how on whales.

HOW WHALES EARN THEIR TITLE OF *ECOSYSTEM ENGINEERS*

The oceans are filled with *phytoplankton*—from Greek words *phyto*: plant, and *plankton*: made to wander or drift, which is precisely what these microscopic plants that live near the water surface do. They absorb carbon dioxide and produce oxygen as a byproduct of photosynthesis—the same as plants on land. Phytoplankton are essential to the marine food chain and in removing carbon dioxide from, and adding oxygen to, the atmosphere. With oceans covering 71% of the Earth's surface (and containing 97% of the Earth's water), it's easy to see the huge role phytoplankton play world-wide.

Here is where blue whales (and other whales as well) come into the picture—specifically, their *fecal plume* or, in plain, unscientific terms—*poop*. And, let's face it, after satisfying its 200-ton body's appetite with a meal of 4 tons of krill (tiny two-inch orange, shrimp-like crustaceans) and digesting it, the blue whale produces ginormous amounts—about 3 tons a day!

A blue whale plunges 500 feet or deeper to dine, then opens its mouth with pleated throat grooves (55-68 pleats extending from the lower jaw to near the navel—yes, it has a belly button as do all mammals) that allow it to expand large enough to take in an amount of water containing krill that equals its own weight: talk about a *Big Gulp!* Then it pushes the water out of its mouth across a baleen filter (bristly plates made of keratin—the same protein material that makes up our hair and fingernails) to strain out the water and keep the krill. The amount of krill a blue whale takes in one mouthful may contain nearly ½ million calories!

In case you're wondering why such a large whale eats such tiny food, here is the reason: while they have very large organs, their esophagus is surprisingly small—only 4 inches in diameter—and, unlike toothed whales that can break up and chew a variety of large oceanic options, the blue whale must swallow its meal whole.

Whales not only need to come to the surface to breathe but, as it turns out, to "go to the bathroom" too: they must shut down that biological function when they dive. What they release is almost in a liquid form that looks like an enormous *orange plume-like cloud* that floats on top of the ocean. The *fecal plume* contains iron and nitrogen, fertilizing the phytoplankton that absorb carbon, produce oxygen, and nourish the krill—the blue whale's food source, which after being digested results in *fecal plumes* that fertilize the phytoplankton. And the cycle continues.

With all their diving, whales push up even more nutrients from the ocean's depth to the surface, helping the phytoplankton flourish: the more phytoplankton, the more carbon dioxide is consumed, oxygen released and, don't forget, food produced for the blue whale's *Big Gulps!*

Switching to the sperm whale's contribution: They dive into very deep water (usually 2,000 to 3,280 feet but as much as 4,000 feet—holding their breath up to 90 minutes!) to feast on iron rich food (a ton a day), and they come back to the surface to breathe and poop, releasing the nutrients that fertilize the phytoplankton. It is estimated that sperm whale poop alone, by fertilizing the carbon-absorbing phytoplankton, might contribute to extracting as much as 450,000 tons of carbon from the atmosphere a year. And because many whales, especially baleen whales like the blue whale, migrate long distances, they generously spread their nutrition-rich, phytoplankton-loving *fecal plumes* everywhere they go!

It's easy to see now that whales are not merely majestic marine mammals that share the world with and intrigue us, but how significant they are in sustaining life on Earth!

> *We have to rethink the ocean.*
> *The ocean is the most important aspect of the Earth.*
> *Our economy, our health, life itself depends on it.*

—Sylvia Earle, Ph.D. Duke University, Marine biologist, explorer (over 7,000 hours underwater), author, named a "Living Legend" by Library of Congress.

A FEW FASCINATING, FUN FACTS ABOUT SEVERAL SPECIES OF WHALES

(1) Bowhead whales can live 200 years. It's a baleen whale, like the blue whale, and the longest-living mammal on Earth. They live in the Arctic Seas and scientists think that living in that harsh environment is the reason for their slow growth rate, older age for reproduction, and longer life. Maybe even the fact that they like to "sing" plays a part in their longevity. Scientists who recorded them said they have a surprisingly varied and constantly changing vocal repertoire—apparently, they even like to *improvise like jazz musicians; the diversity and variability of their songs is rivaled only by a few species of song birds.* A recording contract anyone? They certainly would have a long career!

(2) While bowhead whales may vocalize to their heart's content, the blue whale would win the contest of which one is the loudest: the blue whale can boast of being the loudest creature on Earth: *At 188 decibels, their loudest vocalizations can be heard hundreds of miles away and is louder than a jet, which peaks at only 140 decibels. Human ears cringe at sounds over 120-130 decibels.*

(3) Female humpback whales have *BFFs* who reunite every year. They remember and find each other across the ocean and among other whales. (Talk about a loyal friend!) When they meet, they float along together and do what the females of our species like to do—have a meal and enjoy each other's company.

(4) Whales sleep with one-half of their brain asleep at a time so they can continue returning to the surface to breathe. We can breathe while our conscious mind is asleep: *our subconscious mechanisms have control of this involuntary system. But equipped with a voluntary respiratory system, whales (and dolphins) must keep part of the brain alert to trigger each breath.*

(5) The largest brain of any known creature that has ever lived on Earth belongs to the sperm whale and weighs up to 20 pounds. Their huge head is 1/3 their body length, and besides their brain it contains a large cavity filled with a *yellowish fine oil called spermaceti*, which is how they got their name. The purpose of this unique *spermaceti organ*, which has a volume of at least 530 gallons, is not completely known. One scientific theory is that since the fluid hardens to wax when cold, it assists in altering the whale's buoyancy so it can make extremely deep dives and rise again. It also could play an important role in echolocation.

To nourish their 40- to 50-ton "sleek physique" (which enables them to do very deep diving), sperm whales eat about a ton of food a day, composed mostly of squid, octopus and cuttlefish. Their lower jaw is filled with 20-26 pairs of around 2-pound, 4- to 8-inch cone-shaped teeth that fit into sockets in the upper jaw. While they are the largest living animal with teeth, there is some doubt about their need for them since they're not necessary for feeding on their favorite invertebrate meals. One theory why they have teeth but don't use them for hunting for food could be related to their evolutionary process: as they evolved, they developed different hunting and survival methods where teeth were not necessary; over millions of years, their teeth became less useful as other survival techniques continued to develop and help them thrive. It seems they have no problem swallowing their prey whole—even a 60-foot long giant squid. Sperm whales with no teeth or with broken jaws have been found with a *belly full of squid!*

(6) Whales, dolphins and porpoises are *cetaceans* and, while they all belong to the same family, some of them seem to have a special talent: dolphins, porpoises, beluga whales, and killer whales can imitate the patterns of human speech. *Researchers recently found that a female killer*

whale could copy the phrases "hello," "bye-bye," "Amy," and "one, two, three." The orca could also imitate a wolf's howl, an elephant's trumpeting, and the sounds of a creaking door and a "raspberry." And she reproduced the new sounds quickly, some within the first attempt. When they make "Animals' Got Talent," this orca just might be the big winner for her impressions!

(7) And, speaking of winners, Varvara (Russian for Barbara), a female western gray whale, holds the record for the longest migratory trip by a mammal ever recorded: a round-trip journey of almost 14,000 miles in 172 days, from Russia to Mexico and back. In 2015 a team of researchers from the United States and Russia, using satellite-monitored tags, documented the migration of 3 western North Pacific gray whales, *from their primary feeding ground off Russia's Sakhalin Island across the Pacific Ocean and down the West Coast of the United States to Baja, Mexico,* and only Varvara made mammal migratory history!

In general, gray whales have one of the longest migrations of any mammal, taking an average of 2 to 3 months to complete a round-trip of around 8,000 to 10,000 miles. The only known predators of gray whales are killer whales and humans, who almost brought them to extinction several times. But through an international agreement to stop hunting them, *their number has grown to 26,000, similar to what it was before modern-day whaling. As a result of this population recovery, gray whales were removed from the Endangered Species List in 1994.*

> *If we cannot save the whales from extinction,*
> *we have little hope of saving mankind and the life-supplying biosphere.*

—Sir Peter Markham Scott (1909-1989), British ecologist, painter, writer, ornithologist; one of the world's leading naturalists, and one of the most renowned conservationists of the 20th century.

Statue of Sir Peter Scott at the Wetlands Wildfowl Trust: London Wetland Centre, observing wildlife with a sketch pad in hand.

"Described as the 'father of conservation', he led a campaign for endangered wildlife that captured the imagination of a generation, and inspired many to care about wildlife and the environment long before it became mainstream to do so."

He led expeditions, among them to Antarctica and the Galapagos Islands, wrote 18 books on ornithology and conservation, and also illustrated 20 volumes written by others. He received many honors for his work and was the first Englishman to be knighted (in 1973) for his contributions to conservation.

Charming Hummingbirds

A group of hummingbirds is called a "charm"— how fitting!

It's a fact of life, without the birds and the bees—and other pollinating insects and animals—*the human race and all of Earth's terrestrial ecosystems would not survive: About 80% of all flowering plants and over 75% of crops that provide most of our food depend on animal pollinators.* While birds are not the primary pollinators of our food supply, they are essential pollinators for other critical reasons—including the unique hummingbirds, which you soon will see. But first, a little about these extraordinary, glittering *Flying Jewels* (*Joyas Voladoras*—what early Spanish explorers in South America called them). Their iridescent colors come from feather structure, not pigments, and are created by the way light strikes their feathers.

HUMMINGBIRD HABITATS AND CHARACTERISTICS

Unless you live in or visit these places—the Americas (North, Central or South); Mexico; or the Caribbean Islands—you will never get a personal glimpse of a dazzling hummingbird whizzing by. Their habitat is the Western Hemisphere only—now. However, 30-million-year-old hummingbird fossils have been discovered in Germany and France, leading scientists to believe they once flourished in the Old World—Europe and possibly Asia—before disappearing and reestablishing themselves about 22 million years ago in the New World. Biologists are working to unravel the mystery of why hummingbirds became extinct in the Old World and how they were able to migrate to and thrive in the Americas. So far they have two possible theories for their disappearance: too much competition for food and/or climatic change.

These miniscule birds are majestic in every way but size. Their fragile-looking, tiny bodies (3 to 5 inches) and brain (the size of a pea) belie their remarkable characteristics: acrobatic flying skills, stamina, intelligence, memory, assertive territorial defense tactics, and huge number of species—they are the world's second largest family of birds with over 325 species; the tyrant flycatchers are number one with around 400 species.

Their miniature size also conceals an enormous appetite—they must eat about every 10 to 15 minutes during the day to provide the energy to meet their high metabolic requirements (average heart rate during flight is 1,260 beats per minute). This is where their remarkable memory comes in handy: in order to consume enough for their daily energy needs, they drink nectar (a watery solution of the sugars fructose, glucose, and sucrose) from at least 1,000 flowers a day (plus eat hundreds of small insects for protein and other nutrients), remembering every flower they visit (including those on migration routes) and how long it will be until the flower generates more nectar.

During the night when hummingbirds can't eat, to prevent starvation and keep them alive, they go into a torpor state (short term hibernation) that drastically lowers their heart rate and body temperature to conserve energy. Their "internal clock" begins awakening them 1 to 2 hours before dawn, and it takes from 20 minutes to an hour to fully revive. They lose about 10% of their body weight each night and, of course, the first order of the day is a big breakfast of sucrose! (This is known by the kinds of flowers they prefer—the ones with nectar composed mainly of sucrose.) A hummingbird can consume ½ to twice its weight in one day and will eat around 25% of its daily intake of food as soon as it recovers from torpor.

The poem already mentions their acrobatic abilities, but here are some flying additions: they don't "flap" their wings but rotate them in an *oval pattern* when flying and a *figure 8* when hovering; they beat their wings about 40 to 80 times a second in flight (around 25 to 30 mph) and about 200 times a second when diving (at a speed of 50 to 60 mph); their wings make a "humming" sound, which is how they were named.

While most hummingbird species never venture north from Mexico and Central and South America, about 23 species visit North America during part of the year; around 17 species breed here, migrating back and forth in spring and winter (with just a few species staying in the United States all year). The incredible stamina of these birds becomes apparent when we know that one species, the Ruby-throated Hummingbird, migrates from the eastern United States to its winter home in Mexico or Central America, via the Gulf of Mexico, in an 18- to 22-hour non-stop flight! They "bulk up" to prepare for this journey by doubling their weight.

Another species, the Rufous Hummingbird, weighing in at around 1-1/2 pennies, shows us its hardy side too. Although making stops for "refueling," it travels almost 4,000 miles from its winter home in Mexico to Alaskan breeding grounds in spring, and back to Mexico for the winter—a champion at piling up 8,000 frequent flyer miles every year!

WHY THESE LILLIPUTIAN BIRDS MAKE OLYMPIAN POLLINATORS

7,000 plant species have flowers that have adapted to being pollinated by hummingbirds; of the more than 200 native species of nectar-producing flowering plants in North America, at least 150 species of these flowers are primarily, and in some instances exclusively, pollinated by hummingbirds. "While we may not eat the wildflowers birds pollinate, those plants are important for the health of the global ecosystem as a whole," states Dr. Eugenie Regan, ecologist, researcher, naturalist, and the lead author of a recent study of "Global Trends in the Status of Bird and Mammal Pollinators."

A hummingbird's long beak contains an even longer tongue which allows it to feed at any flower that appeals to it, even those that are too long and thin for anything else to reach the nectar inside.

In fact, their tongue is so long that, when retracted, it coils up inside their head, around their skull and eyes! The birds don't use their beak to "suck out" the nectar as through a straw: their tongue draws liquid into it in a process called "capillary action"— the way water soaks into a paper towel. Once the hummingbird has drunk its fill from a flower and flits off to the next one, the pollen grains that stick to its beak and forehead are transferred; pollination thus occurs if both flowers are the same species. And, because they feed so frequently and reach so many flowers to satisfy their daily requirements, these Lilliputian birds make Olympian pollinators!

The native flowers (also known as wildflowers) that the Rufous and other hummingbirds pollinate when living in or migrating to and from the United States—especially in the Sonoran Desert—not only provide essential hummingbird nourishment and create spectacular landscapes, they have major environmental importance. The Sonoran Desert—an area of over 100,000 square miles located in the southern parts of Arizona and California in the United States, and large parts of the states of Sonora, Baja California Norte and Baja California Sur in Mexico—is known as *one of the most wildly diverse and most ecologically balanced deserts in the world; it plays a big part in the survival of over 500 known species of plants and animals* (emphasis added).

Hummingbird
Sonoran Desert

Photo Credit: Jccv2010

EFFECTS OF A WARMING CLIMATE ON HUMMINGBIRDS

We know our planet has always gone through significant climatic fluctuations over the eons, and while it is true that the Earth currently is in a warming phase, there is not yet complete consensus on all the causes, consequences and solutions. Jon Gertner wants to reassure us that this is not the warning bell for imminent catastrophe in his June 7, 2019 *New York Times* article titled "Maybe We're Not Doomed After All." He writes: *We don't need to assume an attitude of fear and dread. Our scientific progress is a story of technological optimism, defined by an extraordinary sense of capability. It shows what might be built and gained in the coming decades and not merely what could be lost.* Be that as it may, in the meantime there are signs that the little hummingbirds are already being affected—and, of course, not just hummingbirds.

With our climate warming, the wildflowers necessary for hummingbirds' survival are starting to bloom earlier in the Sonoran Desert, as elsewhere. This earlier blossoming creates a mismatch between hummingbird arrival and flourishing flowers, disrupting the established synchronized relationship between these birds and their food source. Known as a *keystone species* (a species on which other species in an ecosystem largely depend, and if they disappeared the ecosystem would be either seriously altered or vanish), hummingbirds are critical for the desert ecosystem, preserving it and their own existence, as well as that of a great number of other animals and plants.

The disappearance of hummingbirds would mean not only the loss of plants that rely on them for pollination but, as disastrous, the non-native plant species that would replace them, which already is occurring in the Sonoran Desert and *could be a forecast of the future elsewhere.*

The menacing Sonoran culprit is *buffelgrass*, which grows in clumps and is native to the savannas in Africa. It was brought to the United States for the purpose of erosion control and use as forage for ranch livestock. However, it is now invading, threatening and out-competing native plants for space, water and nutrients. As if this isn't serious enough, buffelgrass not only thrives on fires that kill native plants, it *can carry a ground fire towards species that are not adapted to survive fire. Its rapid spread is transforming fire-resistant desert into flammable grassland.* With the disappearance of hummingbirds and thriving native plants, the harmful invaders taking over could devastate that ecosystem.

HOW HUMMINGBIRDS ENTER THE GLOBAL PICTURE

Knowing the critical role pollinating animals play in life on Earth, NASA has become involved (in joint efforts with the U.S. Geological Survey, National Park Service, U.S. Fish and Wildlife Service and Smithsonian Institution) *in new research and applications efforts that will bring the global view of climate from space down to Earth to benefit wildlife and key ecosystems. **They are especially interested in hummingbirds because these tiny birds are highly sensitive to climate and weather and are a pioneer indicator of the effects of climate change*** (emphasis added).

This and the following paragraph corroborate the importance of the above research: James W. Cornett (biologist/desert ecologist, author of more than 40 books, and the first professional naturalist to have visited all nine of the world's great deserts) explains that in order for hummingbirds to "maintain [their] unusually high metabolic rates, changes in the gas content of the atmosphere and patterns of plant growth . . . are most likely to affect [them] first. Their fate, in effect, acts as an early warning signal for significant changes in the environment."

The National Audubon Society's scientist, Geoff LeBaron, echoes Cornett's words: Hummingbirds "are a good indication of what's happening with the environment that affects everyone." All of this means, of course, that the inimitable, tiny hummingbird could sadly become the proverbial "canary in the coal mine."

The first step toward change is awareness (Nathaniel Branden), so with the awareness of these issues, better understanding, and the development of sensible strategies, hummingbirds, and all life, should be able to look forward to a bright future. And, as we become more and more aware of hummingbirds and their place in the *Web of Life*, it's easy to agree with Sheri L. Williamson (naturalist, ornithologist, and conservationist) that "hummingbirds have [wide-ranging] impacts far out of proportion to their size."

ONE FINAL FASCINATING FACT
ABOUT THESE FABULOUS FLYING JEWELS

Unlike most birds, hummingbirds do not fly flat, they fly upright, facing the humans with whom they share this *Wonderful World* and to whom they bring such delight!

BUT, BEFORE SAYING *ADIOS* TO THE HUMMINGBIRDS,
LET'S GO DOWN "SOUTH AMERICAN WAY"
(Song by Jimmy McHugh and Al Dubin)

While the focus of this essay has been general hummingbird facts and specifics about those that migrate to and from North America, and their role in flower pollination in this area, the majority of hummingbird habitats are in South America. One of the smallest countries, Ecuador (the size of Colorado), is home to almost half of the over 325 hummingbird species. A fascinating country in itself (its name means equator), the summit of its highest mountain is the place on Earth closest to the sun due to its location along the equatorial bulge. It also is one of the top 10 most biodiverse countries in the world.

An abundance of biodiversity isn't the only unique aspect of Ecuador, but also the number of unusual and rare hummingbirds that can be found there. One of the most distinctive, the Sword-billed Hummingbird, is the only bird in the world with a bill longer than the rest of its body. There is an upside, and a downside, to such an extraordinarily long beak: it gives this species access to the nectar deep in tubular flowers that smaller-beaked hummingbirds are not able to reach, but it also prevents typical avian preening—it is one of the only birds to use its feet for cleaning and grooming its body since its beak is much too long to do the job!

Added to the fascinating hummingbird characteristics already mentioned is another amazing trait of these birds: their ability to live from sea level to the rarified atmosphere of the South American high Andes—some habitats as much as 14,000 feet above sea level. They can live at such high elevations as a result of an adaptation and evolution process that enables them to increase *the oxygen trapping abilities of the hemoglobin in their red blood cells.*

It is precisely in one small spot in the Andes in southwestern Ecuador, at 11,000 feet, that a new hummingbird species was discovered in 2018—the Blue-throated Hillstar with its glittering ultramarine throat. Scientists estimate there are no more than about 300 Blue-throated Hillstars in existence at this time, all living in an isolated 60-square-mile area where their flower preference grows, the Chuquiraga jussieui—known as the *national flower of Andean mountain climbers* and the *flower of true love.*

As exciting and promising as this new hummingbird species is, the researchers who made the discovery have evaluated it as critically threatened and possibly already heading toward extinction because of its endangered habitat. This bird's slightly curved beak is adapted to the Chuquiraga jussieui flower, their main food source that grows in this region, where plant life is being *heavily grazed by cattle and horses and threatened by mining, manmade fires and encroachment from non-native plant species.*

Because of its threatened habitat and diminishing numbers, the Blue-throated Hillstar qualifies for *critically endangered status by International Union for the Conservation of Nature standards.* There are projects underway to educate the local communities in how to protect them by reducing risks of wildfires and other harmful activities. They are also being taught how to create sustainable ecotourism opportunities for viewing this rare bird in its natural habitat.

Before finally allowing all of these "charming" birds to whiz away, let's look at one more unusual hummingbird that is found on the western slopes of the Andes in Ecuador, and a few other South American countries—the Long-tailed Sylph. Unlike the Sword-billed Hummingbird, it has its length at the opposite end—his tail is twice as long as his body. I say "his" since it's only the male with this impressive, iridescent green and blue tail, the purpose of which is the same as that of the peacock's long, showy train. As we might suspect, this hummingbird's long tail does affect flying and he requires strong, inventive aerial skills for survival. And, as with all male hummingbirds, once he's dazzled and won a prospective mate with his whirlwind diving performance (and, for this species, longer tail feathers than his rivals, which signifies how fit he is since he's managed to survive to this point), he's off for his next adventure.

All hummingbird mamas-to-be take a solo parenting role: they build a nest, about the size of half a ping pong ball, lay 2 eggs the size of jelly beans, and sit on them for 2 to 3 weeks—leaving briefly throughout the day to eat. They nurture the fledglings for about 3 weeks until they're capable of flying. Hummingbird mamas then help their petite progeny for about a week when they first leave the nest, still feeding them while showing them how to catch bugs and find nectar. After teaching them these survival basics, mama shoos them off to make their own way in life and she continues on with hers.

Long-tailed Sylph Hummingbirds - Pichincha, Ecuador in the Andean Cloudforest

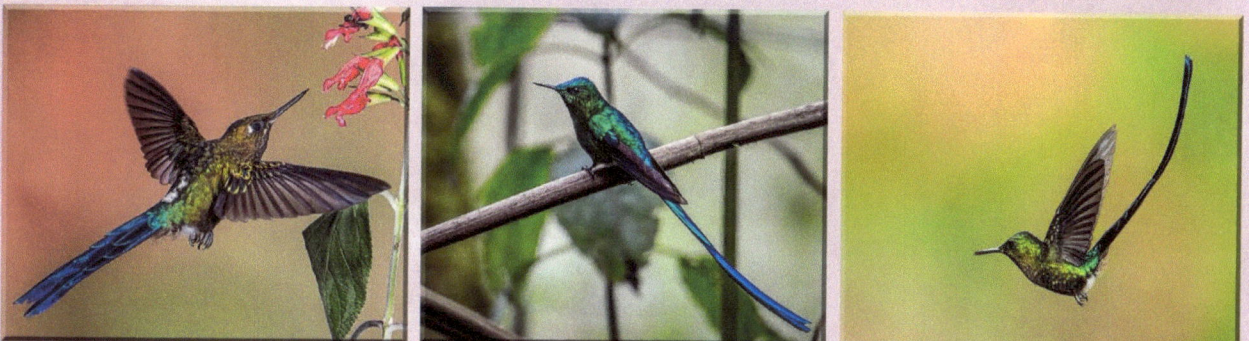

Photo Credit: Andy Morffew

HASTA LA VISTA, HUMMINGBIRDS

I can't think of a more fitting way to say *hasta la vista* to the hummingbirds than with these two stanzas (the first and last) from the poem, "The Humming-Bird," by Mary Botham Howitt (1799-1888). A British author and poet, she never saw a hummingbird in person but, as with so many, she was charmed by these avian jewels. A contemporary of Charles Dickens, Elizabeth Barrett Browning, and William Wordsworth, she was an ardent supporter of the struggle for women's right to vote in Britain, making a name for herself by being an author, translator (she taught herself Swedish and Danish and translated some of Hans Christian Anderson's tales into English) or editor of more than 110 works!

"The Humming-Bird"
by Mary Botham Howitt

The humming-bird! The humming-bird!
So fairy-like and bright;
It lives among the sunny flowers,
A creature of delight!

A reign of summer joyfulness
To thee for life is given;
Thy food, the honey from the flower,
Thy drink, the dew from heaven!

Portrait of young Mary Botham Howitt
"One of the most graceful, versatile and voluminous writers [of her era]."

Author's Note

[As] I think to myself, "What a wonderful world!"
(Song written by George David Weiss, Robert Thiele; Recorded by Louis Armstrong)

Carl Linnaeus (1707-1778), the Swedish scientist who wore many hats (botanist, physician, zoologist, mineralogist), created a classification system for plants and animals which is still used today, with some changes and additions. In 1758 he crowned us with the title Homo sapiens (Latin: Homo, man/human; sapiens, wise), an auspicious name to be sure, which is incumbent upon all of us to live up to. I think the best way we can do this is to be grateful for and learn from the many sources of wisdom passed down through the ages, which have guided us as individuals, families, communities, and residents of this glorious, life-filled world. And, to this we add our own knowledge, experience, and understanding to hopefully increase wisdom for the future.

When, how or why Earth became our "home sweet home" is not a subject for this book, nor is a discussion of environmental suggestions. (There are innumerable wonderful sources, and one I would like to point out is an excellent educational, fun book for children and adults titled NOT YOUR TYPICAL BOOK ABOUT THE ENVIRONMENT by Elin Kelsey, Ph.D.—book's capital letters and underline.) But, we *are* here, and we *are* the ones who know and appreciate how the ecosystem regulates and sustains life on Earth. It is imperative for us Homo sapiens to keep our home healthy, habitable, and enduring. Having knowledge without the wisdom of how to use it for the good of each other, and the world, would be a great injustice to our name and tremendous ingratitude for our extraordinary existence and abilities.

Contrary to Carl Sagan, who refers to our breathtaking Blue Planet as "a mote of dust floating in the morning sky," Marcelo Gleiser, a theoretical physicist, cosmologist and professor of natural philosophy, physics, and astronomy at Dartmouth College, and the 2019 winner of the prestigious Templeton Prize (joining 48 previous honorees, including Mother Teresa, Dalai Lama, King Abdullah II of Jordan, Rabbi Jonathan Sacks, Desmond Tutu, and theoretical physicists Paul Davies and Freeman Dyson), asserts:

We can state, with high confidence, that even if there are other intelligent creatures in the universe, even humanoid ones, they won't be like us. We are the only humans in the cosmos, the product of a very particular set of cosmic, geochemical and evolutionary circumstances. For all practical purposes, we are alone . . . capable of pondering our origins and the future.

This is the striking revelation from modern science, one that should grab everyone's attention. We matter because we are rare and our planet matters because it is unique. Next time you hear a scientist saying something like 'the more we know about the universe the less important we become,' beg to differ. The reality is precisely the opposite: The more we know about the universe, the more unique we become. What we do with this knowledge is, of course, a personal choice for each of us.

https://www.npr.org/sections/13.7/2016/02/03/465401401/evaluating-our-importance-in-the-universe

When I came across the book, *An Ecology of Happiness* by Eric Lambin, it instantly piqued my interest—how could it not! We all are familiar with how majestic mountains, verdant landscapes, lofty trees (Muir Woods for me) can refresh our spirit, but Lambin, a professor in the Stanford School of Earth Sciences and a world leader in the study of land use and human-environment interactions, has a theory that goes beyond this and contends that "human happiness [is] rooted in sustaining the Earth":

The yearning to interact with the natural environment is inscribed in human nature. To preserve the natural world and its diversity is thus in the profound interest of individuals and of humanity. Indeed, respect for the environment is based on an effective connection with nature, and thus contributes to human happiness.

I would like to conclude with some encouraging quotes, beginning with Dr. Patrick Moore, who calls himself a "Greenpeace dropout," 15 years after he helped start it. He says in his book, *Confessions of a Greenpeace Dropout: The Making of a Sensible Environmentalist*, that his transformation came about when he was introduced to the concept of "sustainable development" and saw how the policies of Greenpeace were becoming "extremist and irrational." He states in his book,

[i]n the final analysis, environmentalism should be about learning how to extract the food, energy and materials we need to survive while at the same time reducing our negative environmental impacts as we do so. . . . I believe we can meet these challenges, and I will be the last one to sink into a doomsday funk.

Diane Ackerman, the bestselling author of *The Zookeeper's Wife*, reassures us in her book, *The Human Age: The World Shaped by Us*,

[w]e control our own legacy. We're not passive, we're not helpless. . . . We can become Earth-restorers and Earth-Guardians. We still have time and talent, and we have a great many choices. Our mistakes are legion, but our imagination is immeasurable.

Dr. Robert Pollack, professor of biological sciences at Columbia University, completely agrees:

Our mental capabilities and our capacities for joint action . . . give us a unique extra capacity to control our future, a capacity we do not share with any other known creature on Earth. Let's hope we use that power wisely. (The Faith of Biology and the Biology of Faith)

And finally, Jane Goodall, the world-famous anthropologist, sagely reminds us:

You cannot get through a day without having an impact on the world around you. What you do makes a difference and you have to decide what kind of difference you want to make.

YES, WE *ARE* EACH OTHER'S AND THE WORLD'S KEEPERS!

Additional Notes

"Responsibility is perhaps the most important value parents can teach their children."

This is the statement by William Kilpatrick (M.A. Harvard University—Education; Ph.D. Purdue University—Counseling Psychology) on the cover of Linda and Richard Eyre's book, *Teaching Your Children Responsibility*. The Eyres have written over a dozen books on parenting and values, and their 1993 book, *Teaching your Children Values*, was the first parenting book to reach #1 on the *New York Times Book Review* bestseller list since 1946—Dr. Benjamin Spock's *Baby and Child Care*.

While living a responsible life encompasses all aspects of personal behavior and accountability that are essential for a good individual and communal life, in this book I have chosen to stress two—kindness to each other and the Earth—which are integral to *tikkun olam*, making the world a better place. Interestingly, the term *tikkun olam* and its message were brought to international public attention at a meeting in Miami in 1987, with Pope John Paul II in attendance.

In 2014 Jonathan Krasner wrote, in an article for The Jerusalem Center for Public Affairs, that "[t]he symbolic moment when the now ubiquitous phrase *tikkun olam* entered the . . . mainstream probably took place during the visit of Pope John Paul II to the United States. Rabbi Mordecai Waxman, chairman of the International Jewish Committee on Interreligious Consultations, addressing the Pope in his speech, stated: 'Your presence here in the United States affords us the opportunity to reaffirm our commitment to the sacred imperative of *tikkun olam*, the mending of the world.'"

The following words from the Eyres' book on responsibility very well could be the mantra for raising children to become responsible adults: "Responsibility is not the result of maturity, but the cause of it." Their emphasis on how "our actions affect others" definitely can't be highlighted enough.

Dr. James Roswell Gallagher (1903-1995), *credited with shaping adolescent medicine into a recognized discipline*, expressed the value of kindness this way: "Kindness antedates psychiatry by hundreds of years; its antiquity should not lessen your opinion of its usefulness . . . [and] the same can be said of the Bible and wise individuals." Wisdom, wherever it's gleaned, is timeless; examples that have a connection to the ideas in this book are on the last page.

Gail Lynne Goodwin, in her essay "Kindness: The Core of 12 Religions," calls kindness the "universal language that all people understand." Alonzo Smith "Jake" Gaither (1903-1994), head football coach at Florida A&M University from 1945 to 1969, said the football field was "his laboratory for manhood," stressing character over talent. Rachel Naomi Remen, M.D., in her book *Kitchen Table Wisdom*, couldn't agree more: "[T]he worth of any lifetime is measured more in kindness than in competency."

Actions speak louder than words may be a well-worn maxim, but many a truth and much wisdom are found in oft-repeated aphorisms and age-old proverbs. Sophocles' words that the act of "kindness begets kindness evermore" go back a lot farther than the motto at the beginning of this paragraph. One more noteworthy ancient source of wisdom, the Talmud, teaches:

"The highest form of wisdom is kindness."

I can't think of a better way to end this book (please see the last page also) than with the words below, which resonate so deeply with me and perfectly express the guiding precept of *tikkun olam*—repairing the world—"for every generation":

I shall pass through this world but once. Any good therefore that I can do or any kindness that I can show to any human being, let me do it now. Let me not defer or neglect it, for I shall not pass this way again.

—Stephen Gellet
French-born American Quaker missionary
1773-1855

If we can incorporate the wise words of these individuals, from various philosophical, scientific, theological, and other backgrounds, into our daily lives, I believe we will have a good chance to help make "our World the Greatest Home for every generation."
(Listed in chronological birth dates, except for the last one which is date of quote.)

The beginning is the most important part of the work.
Plato (circa 428 BCE)

It is not your responsibility to finish the work of perfecting the world, but you are not free to desist from it either.
Rabbi Tarfon in the *Ethics of the Fathers* (between 70 CE and 135 CE)

Nature-study gives the child a sense of companionship with life. If a teacher walks with [children] in paths that lead to the seeing and comprehending of what is beneath [their] feet or above [their] head, these paths . . . finally converge and bring the wanderer to that serene peace and hopeful faith that is the sure inheritance of all those who realize fully that they are working units of this wonderful universe.
Anna Botsford Comstock (1854-1930)
(She completed her degree in natural history in 1885; was first female professor at Cornell; wrote *The Handbook of Nature Study* in 1911— still in print and considered a standard textbook.)

We must never permit the voice of humanity within us to be silenced. It is man's sympathy with all creatures that first makes him truly a man.
Dr. Albert Schweitzer (1875-1965)

We are at the very beginning of time for the human race. It is not unreasonable that we grapple with problems. . . .

Our responsibility is to do what we can, learn what we can, improve the solutions, and pass them on.
Physicist Richard P. Feynman, Ph.D. (1918-1988)

The time is always right to do what is right.
Reverend Dr. Martin Luther King, Jr. (1929-1968)

Today, more than ever before, life must be characterized by a sense of Universal responsibility, not only nation to nation and human to human, but also human to other forms of life.
Dalai Lama (1935)

Humans aren't as good as we should be in our capacity to empathize with feelings and thoughts of others, be they humans or other animals on Earth. So maybe part of our formal education should be training in empathy. Imagine how different the world would be if, in fact, there were 'reading, writing, arithmetic, empathy.'
Astrophysicist Neil deGrasse Tyson, Ph.D. (1958)

Responsibility is more important than any one subject a person can learn in school. Without responsibility a person cannot succeed in any subject or in life.
Ridgewood High School student
Jerry Leibfritz, Norridge, Illinois
Nominee for the *Chicago Tribune* Illinois High School All-State Academic Team (1987)